THE PORTABLE CRAFTER
CROSS-STITCH

THE PORTABLE CRAFTER
CROSS-STITCH

Liz Turner Diehl

Sterling Publishing Co., Inc.
New York
A Sterling/Chapelle Book

Chapelle, Ltd., Inc.,

P.O. Box 9252, Ogden, UT 84409

(801) 621-2777 • (801) 621-2788 Fax

e-mail: chapelle@chapelleltd.com

Web site: www.chapelleltd.com

Library of Congress Cataloging-in-Publication Data

Diehl, Liz Turner.
  The portable crafter: cross-stitch/Liz Turner Diehl.
    p. cm.
  Includes index
  ISBN 1-4027-2140-4
    1. Cross-stitch. I. Title.
  TT778.C76D54   2006
  746.44'3--dc22   2005018797

Published by Sterling Publishing Co., Inc.
387 Park Avenue South, New York, NY 10016
©2006 by Liz Turner Diehl
Distributed in Canada by Sterling Publishing
c/o Canadian Manda Group, One Atlantic Avenue, Suite 105
Toronto, Ontario, Canada M6K 3E7
Distributed in Great Britain by Chrysalis Books Group PLC,
The Chrysalis Building, Bramley Road, London W10 6SP, England
Distributed in Australia by Capricorn Link (Australia) Pty. Ltd.
P.O. Box 704, Windsor, NSW 2756, Australia
Printed in China
All Rights Reserved

Sterling ISBN 1-4027-2140-4

For information about custom editions, special sales, premium
and corporate purchases, please contact Sterling Special Sales
Department at 800-805-5489 or specialsales@sterlingpub.com.

TABLE OF CONTENTS

INTRODUCTION

Cross-stitch is the craft of needle arts embellishing even-weave fabric with glorious design to pleasure the senses. Counted cross-stitch is the process of application for transferring a design from the paper pattern to the evenweave fabric through stitches that look like an "x."

This style of Danish counted cross-stitch was introduced to the United States in the late 1970s by Ginnie Thompson from Pawleys Island, South Carolina.

Textile needle arts have been around for centuries. The stitches just continue to evolve and the design style changes with the times. Needlework can be divided into three basic forms: surface work, openwork, and raised work. Traditional cross-stitch would be categorized as surface work. The

cross-stitches simply cover the surface to create the design element.

During the 17th century in England, needlework was an important part of a young girl's training. She would begin with surface work, using neutral or white thread and practicing perfect stitches while creating an alphabet sampler, then progress to using colorful silks. As her studies in needlework continued, she learned the technique for achieving beautiful decorative stitches, then added the element of working on canvas and adding beads. Next, her studies took her into the world of open-work to learn the techniques of drawn thread and pulled thread. With great interest in style and form and the beauty of needlework, she found herself fashioning creations using raised work. The most popular of this era, raised work created dimension in the needlework through the use of padding, stuffing, and wired techniques. It was not until the late 1800s that this style of raised embroidery from the mid 1600s was coined "stumpwork." Stumpwork is a modern term, its first known use being in 1894. History books speculate on its origin. Phrases such as "work on the stamp" and "work on the stump" are possibilities. The French work "estompe," meaning embossed, is thought to have a correlation today. Stumpwork is a term used to define raised or padded needlework.

History shows that needlework is an important part of culture and greatness is achieved by both men and woman, young and old.

This book is filled with cross-stitch projects that make great gifts, as well as things for you to enjoy. The best part is that they are all easy and fun to make on the go.

Floral Bracelet on page 50

CROSS-STITCH BASICS

The projects in *The Portable Crafter: Cross-Stitch* were selected so that you can work on them while you are on the go, on a roadtrip, waiting at the doctor's office, or in the carpool line. However, with any project there are some cross-stitch basics that should be considered before you step out of the door.

These basics are found on pages 9–19. Information such as threads, cross-stitch fabrics, supplies, terms to know, and stitches to know will aid in creating the projects featured in this book. While this book is in the *Portable Crafter* series, it is best to spend a little time in preparation such as gathering the materials and ironing any ribbons and/or fabrics.

English Knot Garden on page 53

THREADS

Besides the design itself no other element defines a cross-stitch project as much as the threads used to create the design. Different threads offer variety of sheen, thickness, and texture. The type and color of threads used in each project have been provided for your convenience. However, feel free to use any desired type or desired color.

Most numbers and color names on the codes represent the Madeira brand of thread. Use 18" lengths of thread. For best coverage, separate the strands and dampen with a wet sponge, then put together the number of strands required for the fabric used.

Embroidery Floss

Embroidery floss is a six-ply cotton with sheen. It is best to separate the piles as stated above, then recombined the strands, creating a fuller look. (Photo 1)

Photo 1

Photo 2

Pearl Cotton

Cotton is washable and easy to work with, but does not wear as well as wool. Pearl cotton is twisted, nonseparable, and has a lustrous sheen. (Photo 2)

Rayon

Rayon thread is smooth and silky, with a radiant sheen. These threads can be difficult to work with because they easily kink and knot. Dampen the threads for ease of stitching.

Metallic

Metallic threads resemble a string of tiny beads. These threads can be used alone or combined with other fibers.

Silk

Smoother, stronger, and more expensive than cotton, the structure of the silk thread enables it to reflect light in a distinctive way. It glides easily through the fabric. Silk threads come in weights similar to cotton threads.

Blending

Blending threads are often combined with other fibers, creating highlights for special effects. (Photo 3)

Photo 3

Counted cross-stitch is worked on even-weave fabrics. These fabrics are manufactured specifically for counted-thread embroidery, and are woven with the same number of vertical as horizontal threads per inch (Photo 4)

Because the number of threads in the fabric is equal in each direction, each stitch will be the same size. The number of threads per inch in even-weave fabrics determines the size of a finished design.

Photo 4

Linen cross-stitch fabric has the appearance, strength, and longevity to make it a popular choice for stitchers for counted cross-stitch.

Aida cross-stitch fabric has small corner holes that make counting easier and enable the stitcher to see exactly where each stitch should be placed. Aida fabrics are usually chemically sized by the manufacturer to impart stiffness to the fabric.

SUPPLIES

Embroidery Scissors

Embroidery scissors are used for trimming threads and floss. Use the embroidery scissors for needlework only. Avoid using the tip of the embroidery scissors to cut metallic threads, use the area of the blade closer to the base.

Needles

Needles come in a variety of kinds and sizes. The needles used in this book are chenille, beading, and tapestry. Chenille needles have sharp pointed ends with large eyes for easily threading.

Beading needles are very fine, long needles with a long narrow eye that can pass easily through the hole of beads.

Tapestry needles are blunt-pointed needles that are useful when you need to weave an additional thread on the surface of already-completed stitches. For fabric with 11 or fewer threads per inch, use a tapestry needle size 24; for 14 threads per inch, use a tapestry needle size 24, 26, or 28; for 18 or more threads per inch, use a tapestry needle size 26 or size 28. Avoid leaving the needle in the design area of the fabric. It may leave a rust mark or a permanent impression on the fabric.

Embellishments

Embellishments are a way to add that something extra to a cross-stitch project. Beads, crystals, and tassels are all wonderful ways to enhance a design. (Photos 4, 5, and 6) Using such wonderful embellishments can only make a piece of hand-crafted work all the more special.

CROSS-STITCH ITEMS TO KNOW

Number of Floss Strands

The number of floss strands used per stitch varies, depending on the fabric used. Generally, the rule to follow for cross-stitching is three strands of floss on Aida 11, two strands on Aida 14, one or two strands on Aida 18 (depending on desired thickness of stitches), and one strand on Hardanger 22.

For backstitching, use one strand on all fabrics. When completing a French Knot (FK), use one strand and one wrap on all fabrics, unless otherwise directed.

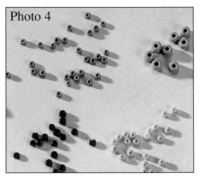

Photo 4

Photo 5

Photo 6

Finished Design Size

To determine the size of the finished design, divide the stitch count by the number of threads per inch of fabric. When a design is stitched over two threads, divide the stitch count by half the threads per inch. For example, if a design with a stitch count of 120 width and 250 height was stitched on a 28-count linen (over two threads, making it 14 count), the finished size would be 8⅝" x 17⅞".

120 ÷ 14" = 8⅝" (width)

250 ÷ 14" = 17⅞" (height)

Finished size = 8⅝" x 17⅞"

Preparing Fabric

Cut fabric at least 3" larger on all sides than the finished design size to ensure enough space for desired assembly. To prevent fraying, whipstitch or machine-zigzag along the raw edges or apply liquid fray preventive.

Centering Design on Fabric

Fold the fabric in half horizontally, then vertically. Place a pin in the intersection to mark the center. Locate the center of the design on the graph. To help in centering the designs, gold dots are provided at the center top and bottom and center sides. Begin stitching all designs at the center point of the graph and fabric.

Securing Floss

Insert needle up from the underside of the fabric at starting point. Hold 1" of thread behind the fabric and stitch over it, securing with the first few stitches. To finish thread, run under four or more stitches on the back of the design. Avoid knotting floss, unless working on clothing.

Another method of securing floss is the waste knot. Knot floss and insert needle down from the top left side of the fabric about 3" from the design area. Work the area. Cut off the knot, rethread the needle and secure thread under worked stitches.

Carrying Floss

To carry floss, run floss under the previously worked stitches on the back. Do not carry thread across any fabric that is not or will not be stitched. Loose threads, especially dark ones, will show through the fabric.

Cleaning Finished Design

When stitching is finished, soak the fabric in cold water with a mild soap for 5–10 minutes. Rinse well and roll in a towel to remove excess water. Do not wring. Place the piece face down on a dry towel and iron on a warm setting until the fabric is dry.

Fleur-de-lis Tassel on page 42

Fleur-de-lis Tassel on page 42

TRAVEL & STITCHING HINTS

- Keep adhesive notepads on hand to underline areas on the chart as you stitch.

- Highlight chart areas that have just been stitched with colored markers.

- Good lighting is key to an enjoyable stitching experience. When on the go, travel with a portable light available in your local needlework store or office supply store. Some models offer a powerful magnifying lens. Portable around-the-neck magnifiers are also available. Hotels outfit their rooms with mood lighting. Pick up the phone and request a 100-watt lightbulb from housekeeping. They are usually very accommodating. Or, add a bright lightbulb, for an emergency, to your stitching basket.

- Thread organizers come in many styles. They help to control your bundle of threads.

- If you enjoy using an embroidery hoop to stretch your

fabric, remove the fabric from the hoop after each stitching session. This will eliminate permanent creases and soiling. To enjoy easier thread movement, place the screw pin of the hoop to a position of 10 o'clock if you are right-handed and to the position of 2 o'clock if you are left-handed. This will keep the screw pin out of the way of your stitching.

- A small needle case with magnets is a great way to store your needles and embroidery scissors when creating these projects on the go. (Photo 7)

Photo 7

Backstitch (BS)

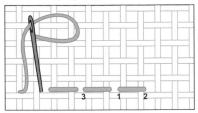

Bead Attachment Stitch (BD)

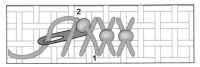

Buttonhole Stitch (BH)

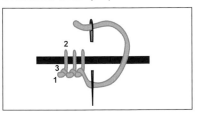

Cashmere Stitch (CS)

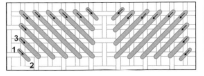

Couch Stitch (CS)

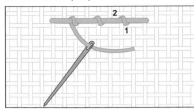

French Knot (FK)

Cross-stitch (XS)

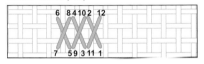

Half-cross Stitch (HX)

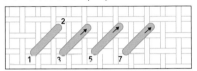

Eyelet Stitch (ES)

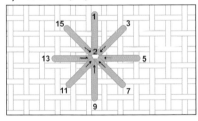

Hungarian Stitch (HS)

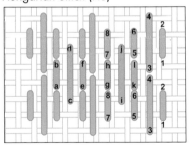

Fan Stitch (FS)

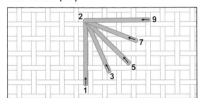

Kloster Block (KB)

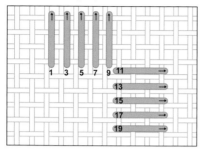

Leaf Stitch (LF)

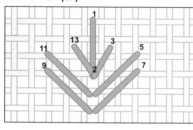

Long Stitch (LS)

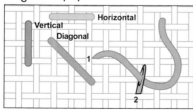

Plait Stitch Variation 1 (PS1)

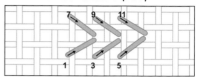

Plait Stitch Variation 2 (PS2)

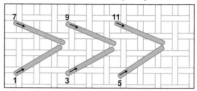

Rice Stitch (RS)

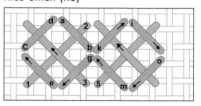

Satin Stitch (SS)

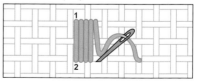

18

Scotch Stitch (SC)

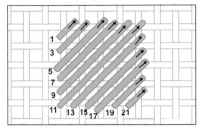

Smyrna Cross-stitch (SX)

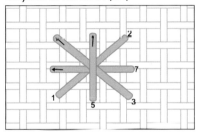

Spider Stitch (SP)

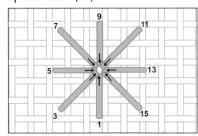

Tied Oblong Cross-stitch (OX)

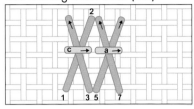

Turkeywork Stitch (TS)

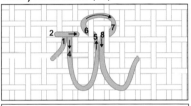

Tip: Work the Turkeywork stitch from bottom to top rows to keep loops out of the way. Tighten each stitch after Step 4. The size of the loops determines the depth of the pile.

FRAMED ACORN

MATERIALS TO GATHER

- 6" x 7" 28-count natural linen
- Embroidery scissors
- Frame as desired
- Needles:
  Beading
  Size 24 tapestry
- Size 8 bronze seed beads (24)

- Threads:
  DMC pearl cotton #435, golden brown
  Madeira cotton #2006, dk. brown (1 skein)
  Madeira cotton #2114, gold (1 skein)
  Madeira rayon #1558, copper (1 skein)

INSTRUCTIONS

Finished size: 1¾" x 2¼"

Note: For stitch types and placements, see the project code and chart on pages 22–23. Each square of the graphed chart represents 1 thread of linen.

1. For stem, cross-stitch 2 stitches at the tip over 2 threads with 3 strands of dk. brown. Refer to Cross-stitch on page 17. Tied oblong cross-stitch over 2 with 3 strands of gold. Refer to Tied Oblong Cross-stitch on page 19.

2. For cap, backstitch the first row with 1 strand of dk. brown. Refer to Backstitch on page 16. *Note: All the stitching for the cap is done with 3 strands of dk. brown.* Plait-stitch the next row, variation 1. Refer to Plait Stitch on page 18. Plait-stitch the next row, variation 2.

Half-cross stitch over 2 threads with dk. brown. Refer to Half-cross Stitch on page 17. Then oblong cross-stitch as shown.

Skip a row. *Note: This is will be a row of beads.* Scotch-stitch the next row reversed over 4 threads as shown. Refer to Scotch Stitch on page 19. *Note: The last two rows are for the Turkeywork. These rows and the row of beads are stitched after all other stitching is complete.*

3. For leaf, backstitch the outer row of the leaf over 2 threads with 3 strands of dk. brown as shown. Backstitch the inner row of the leaf over 2 threads with 3 strands of gold as shown. Backstitch the leaf's vein over 2 threads with 2 strands of copper as shown.

4. Backstitch the acorn's shape over 2 threads with 1 strand of golden brown. Hungarian-stitch to fill in the acorn with 1 strand of golden brown as shown. Refer to Hungarian Stitch on page 17.

5. Turkeywork-stitch the last two rows of acorn with all strands of dk. brown. Refer to Turkeywork Stitch on page 19.

6. Using bead attachment stitch, attach beads onto the next row as shown. Refer to Bead Attachment Stitch on page 16.

7. Frame as desired.

Stitch count: 48 x 65

Madeira Floss										
	XS	**BS**	**OX**	**PS1**	**PS2**	**HX**	**HS**	**SS**	**TW**	**BD**
2114		⌐	✕							
2006	▲	⌐	✕	〉	〉	╱		⁄⁄⁄	‿	
*1558		⌐								
**435		⌐					┆┆┆			
***Bronze										●
*Madeira Rayon **DMC Pearl Cotton ***Size 8 seed bead										

Framed Acorn

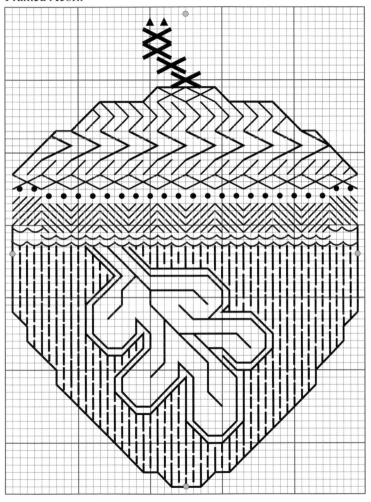

ACORN TASSEL

MATERIALS TO GATHER

- 4" sq. 28-count natural raw linen
- 4" sq. backing fabric
- Bronze seed beads (1 pkg.)
- Embroidery scissors
- Glue
- Size 24 tapestry needle

- Size 45 metal half-ball button covers (2)
- Tassel as desired
- Threads:
  DMC pearl cotton #435, dk. gold
  Madeira cotton #1509 sage green (1 skein)
  Madeira cotton #2203 gold (1 skein)

INSTRUCTIONS

Finished size: 1⅛"

Note: For stitch types and placements, see the project code and charts on pages 27–28. Each square of the graphed chart represents 1 thread of linen.

1. Backstitch the outline of the acorn cap with 1 strand of green cotton as shown on Acorn Tassel 1 on page 28. Refer to Backstitch on page 16.

2. Backstitch the outline of the acorn with 1 strand of gold.

3. Stitch horizontal long stitches in acorn with all 6 strands of gold cotton as shown on Acorn Tassel 2 on page 28. Refer to Long Stitch on page 18.

4. Stitch vertical long stitches over entire acorn with all strands of gold cotton as shown on Acorn Tassel 3 on page 28.

5. Fill the acorn cap with seed beads as shown on Acorn Tassel 4 on page 28. Pile the beads on top of one another to create dimension.

6. *Note: The metal button cover comes in two parts. One is the button cap with teeth and the other part is the button disk that secures the fabric in place. The button cap has a shank which allows you to use this as a button by sewing it onto pillow or garment.* To cover the button, center the stitched design over the cap. Wrap the fabric around the cap and attach the fabric to the teeth. If recentering is needed, lift from the teeth and recenter. Trim away excess fabric around the button, leaving just enough fabric to tuck into the cap.

7. When satisfied with the centering, then push the disk into the back of the cap. *Note: The disk will pop into place, securing and finishing the button.* Cover the button back with the backing fabric.

7. Make tassel hanger with 5 pearl cotton in dk. gold, using the Twisted Cord Technique as follows:

   a. Calculate the length of hanger needed by twisting by multiplying the finished length desired by seven.

   b. Fold the entire length in thirds. Tie a knot at each end. Insert a pencil in front of knots at each end. *Note: This will require two people.*

   c. Stand facing each other, keeping the thread taut at all times. Each person begins turning their pencil in a clockwise direction. Turn the pencils until the thread is twisted so tightly that it begins to double back on itself just near the pencils.

   d. When twisting is complete, find the center of the thread. One person holds the center while the other person pulls the two pencils together, keeping the thread taut. See Diagram A.

Diagram A

e. After the pencils are joined, the center person begins to let go, a few inches at a time. See Diagram B. *Note: The thread will naturally twist itself.*

Diagram B

f. Once you have reached the pencils, remove the pencils and tie all of the ends in one knot.

8. Cut twisted cord into two pieces: one for the desired hanger length and one to glue around the covered button. For the hanger, make a loop out of the twisted cord, place between the two halves of the buttons and glue in place.

9. Wrap and glue another piece of pearl cotton around the edge of the button halves for a finished look.

Stitch count: 22 x 31

Madeira Floss				
	XS	**BS**	**LS**	**BD**
2203		⌐┐	—	
2203			│	
1509	▲	⌐┐		
Bronze				●

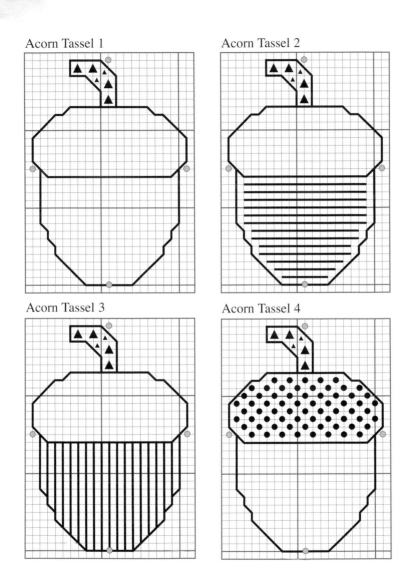

Acorn Tassel 1

Acorn Tassel 2

Acorn Tassel 3

Acorn Tassel 4

DICE POUCH

MATERIALS TO GATHER

- ½"-wide sheer sage ribbon (1 yd)

- 9" x 14" 28-count sky blue even-weave fabric

- 9" x 14" backing fabric

- 5mm faceted round fire-polished clear crystals (15)

- Embroidery scissors

- Size 26 tapestry needle

- Threads:
  Madeira cotton #0706, dk. raspberry (1 skein)
  Madeira cotton #0707, med. raspberry (1 skein)
  Madeira cotton #1214, med. green (1 skein)
  Madeira cotton #1302, dk. green (1 skein)

Madeira cotton #2505, dk. blue (1 skein)
Madeira cotton #2506, med. blue (1 skein)
Madeira cotton #2400, black (1 skein)
Madeira cotton #2401, white (1 skein)
Rainbow blending #R201, turquoise metallic (1 bobbin)
Rainbow blending #R204, green metallic (1 bobbin)
Rainbow blending #R618, raspberry metallic (1 bobbin)

INSTRUCTIONS

Finished size: 5" x 6¼"

Note: For stitch types and placements, see the project code and charts on pages 30–35. Each square of the graphed charts represents 2 threads of the fabric.

1. Cross-stitch with 2 strands of cotton plus 1 strand of blending thread metallic as shown. Refer to Cross-stitch on page 17. Backstitch lettering with 1 strand of black as shown. Refer to Backstitch on page 16.

29

2. Using bead attachment stitch, attach crystals to top side of dice as shown. Refer to Bead Attachment Stitch on page 16.

3. Trim the finished cross-stitch fabric and the backing fabric, leaving a 1" seam allowance on three sides: left side, right side, and bottom. Prefinish the left and right sides of both fabrics by turning the fabric back ⅛" and sewing down.

4. Beginning with the cross-stitch fabric first, fold the top of the fabric to the back. *Note: Folding the fabric back will allow for a ruffle across the top and the header area to thread the drawstring ribbon.* Make certain the fold is deep enough to be able to stitch through both layers for the drawstring ribbon area. Stitch 2 rows of long stitches across the fabric, wide enough for the ribbon to slip through. Repeat for the backing fabric.

5. With right sides together and using a ⅝" seam allowance, stitch from the bottom drawstring ribbon, long stitch down one side, across the bottom and back up the other side. Refer to Long Stitch on page 18. Turn bag right side out.

Stitch count: 75 x 97

Madeira Floss	XS	BS	BD
2401	·		
{ 0707 *R618	+		
{ 0706 *R618	●		
{ 2506 *R201	◇		
{ 2505 *R201	▼		
{ 1214 *R204	○		
{ 1302 *R204	★		
2400	■	⌐	
**Crystals			●

* GlissenGloss Rainbow Blending Thread

**5mm faceted round fire-polished clear crystals

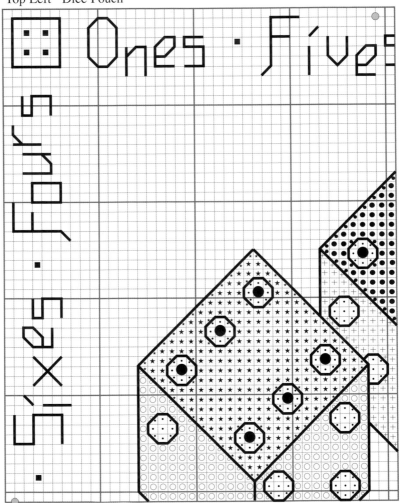

Ones · Fives

Sixes · Fours

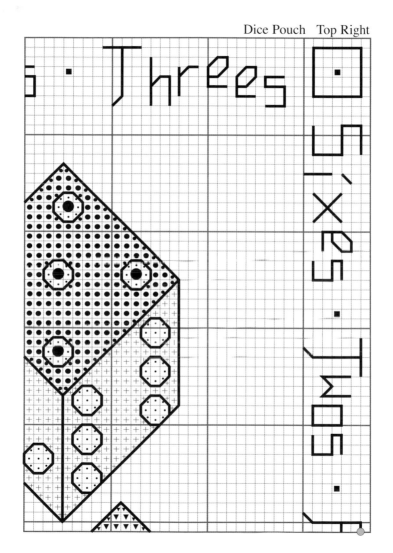

33

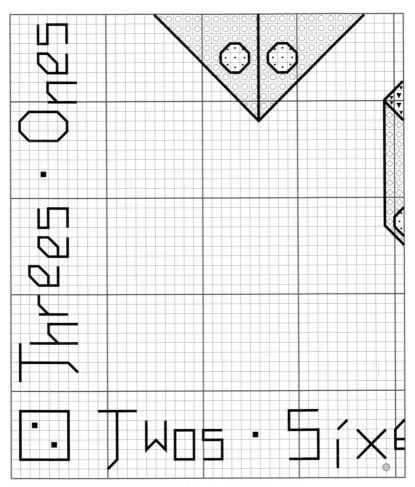

Bottom Left   Dice Pouch

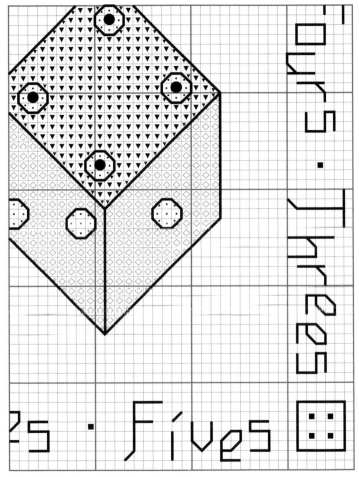

Dice Pouch   Bottom Right

Poker Chip Box

MATERIALS TO GATHER

- 3½" x 4¾" foam-core board
- 8" x 9" 28-count cream linen
- Compressed quilt batting
- Embroidery scissors
- Poker chip box
- Size 24 tapestry needle
- Threads:
  Madeira cotton #0109, yellow (1 skein)

Madeira cotton #0510, red (1 skein)
Madeira cotton #1011, blue (1 skein)
Madeira cotton #2209, gold (1 skein)
Madeira cotton #2400, black (1 skein)
Rainbow blending #R407, metallic gold (1 bobbin)

INSTRUCTIONS

Finished size: 3½" x 4¾"

Note: For stitch types and placements, see the project code and chart on pages 37–38. Each square of the graphed chart represents 2 threads of linen.

1. Cross-stitch with 2 strands of cotton as shown. Refer to Cross-stitch on page 17. To add blending thread, use 2 strands of cotton plus 1 strand of blending thread.

2. Backstitch with 1 strand of black. Refer to Backstitch on page 16.

3. Place a piece of compressed quilt batting on top of foam-core board, creating padding. Trim batting to the same size as the board. Do not wrap around the edges.

4. Center and place the finished cross-stitch design on top of the batting. On the back side, stitch back and forth, side to side, like lacing a shoe, while pulling and

centering the cross-stitch design as you go.

5. Glue to top of box.

6. Create a twisted cord with black strands, using the Twisted Cord Technique, Step 7 on pages 26–27.

7. Glue the twisted cord to the outside edge of the finished cross-stitch design. Tie a bow at one or both ends as desired.

Stitch count: 44 x 59

Madeira Floss		
	XS	**BS**
0109	⊞	
{ 2209 *R407	▼	
0510	●	
1011	△	
2400	E	⌐
*GlissenGloss Rainbow Blending Thread		

Poker Chip Box

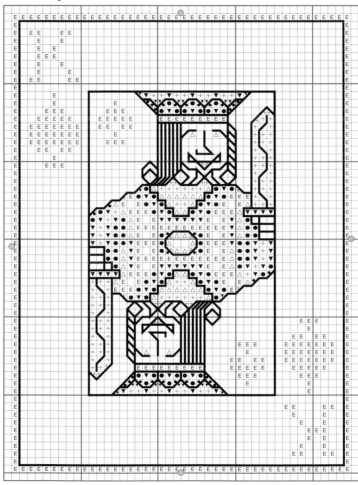

BRIDGE BOX

- 3½" x 4¾" foam-core board
- 8" x 9" 28-count cream linen
- Bridge box
- Compressed quilt batting
- Embroidery scissors
- Size 24 tapestry needle
- Threads:
  Madeira cotton #0109, yellow (1 skein)

Madeira cotton #0510, red (1 skein)
Madeira cotton #1011, blue (1 skein)
Madeira cotton #2209, gold (1 skein)
Madeira cotton #2400, black (1 skein)
Rainbow blending #R407, metallic gold (1 bobbin)

Finished size: 3½" x 4¾"

Note: For stitch types and placements, see the project code and chart on pages 40–41. Each square of the graphed chart represents 2 threads of linen.

1. Cross-stitch with 2 strands of cotton as shown. Refer to Cross-stitch on page 17. To add the blending thread, use 2 strands of cotton plus 1 strand of the blending thread.

2. Backstitch with 1 strand of black. Refer to Backstitch on page 16.

3. Place a piece of compressed quilt batting on top of foam-core board, creating padding. Trim batting to the same size as the board. Do not wrap around the edges.

4. Center and place the finished cross-stitch design on top of the batting. On the backs side,

39

stitch back and forth, side to side, like lacing a shoe, while pulling and centering the cross-stitch design as you go.

5. Glue to top of box.

6. Create a twisted cord with black strands, using the Twisted Cord Technique, Step 7 on pages 26–27.

7. Glue the twisted cord to the outside edge of the finished cross-stitch design. Tie a bow at one or both ends as desired.

Stitch count: 44 x 59

Madeira Floss		
	XS	**BS**
0109	+	
{ 2209 { *R407	▼	
0510	●	
1011	△	
2400	E	⌐
*GlissenGloss Rainbow Blending Thread		

Bridge Box

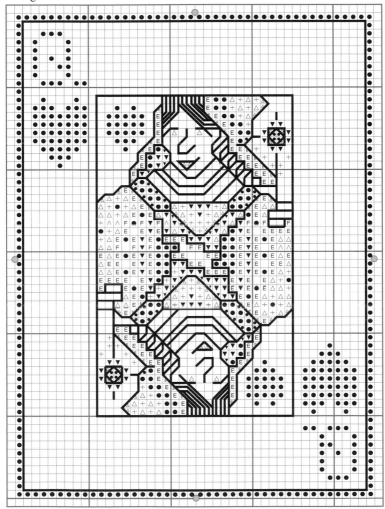

Fleur-de-lis Tassel

- 6" sq. 25-count antique white linen
- 13½" sq. finished pillow
- Embroidery scissors
- Size 24 tapestry needle
- Size 100 metal half-ball button cover
- Tassel as desired

- Threads:
  Madeira silk #2209, gold (1 skein)
  Madeira metallic #9805 -5014, antique gold (1 skein)
  Madeira lacquered jewel #J424, antique gold (1 bobbin)

INSTRUCTIONS

Finished size: 2½"

Note: For stitch types and placements, see the project code and charts on pages 44–46. Each square of the graphed chart represents 1 thread of linen.

1. Backstitch the fleur-de-lis the outline with 1 strand of gold silk as shown. Refer to Backstitch on page 16.

2. Backstitch the design 1 over 1 with gold silk as shown.

3. Fill in fleur-de-lis, using vertical and diagonal long stitches with 4 strands of gold silk as shown. Refer to Long Stitch on page 18.

4. Lay down 1 strand of the metallic antique gold over the backstitching lines all around the fleur-de-lis. Couch-stitch metallic floss to the linen with 1 strand of antique gold metallic. Refer to Couch Stitch on page 17.

5. Stitch the tie that holds the fleur-de-lis together in the

42

middle. Begin with stitching vertical long stitches over existing stitches to help pad the area with 1 strand of antique gold metallic as shown.

6. Stitch horizontal long stitches over the area with the same metallic gold, creating a look of a tie around the middle as shown on Fleur-de-lis Tassel 2 on page 46.

7. Using the metal button as a template, cut the design out in the circular shape, leaving a 1" seam allowance. *Note: It is better to cut the circle a little on the larger size first. Additional trimming may always be done.*

8. *Note: The metal button cover comes in two parts. One is the button cap with teeth and the other part is the button disk that secures the fabric in place. The button cap has a shank which allows you to use this as a button by sewing it onto pillow or garment.* To cover the button, center the stitched design over the cap. Wrap the fabric around the cap and attach the fabric to the teeth. If it needs recentering, lift from the teeth and recenter. Trim away excess fabric around the button, leaving just enough fabric to tuck into the cap.

9. When satisfied with the centering, then push the disk into the back of the cap. *Note: The disk will pop into place, securing and finishing the button.* Using the shank at the back of the button, stitch the button and tassel to the finished pillow.

Stitch count: 44 x 43

Madeira Silk			
	BS	**LS**	**LS**
2209			
*9805			
*Madeira Metallic			

Fleur-de-lis Tassel 1

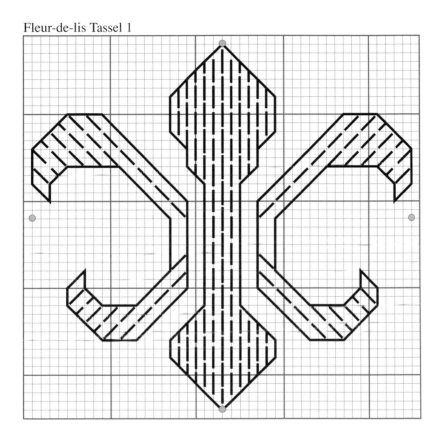

Fleur-de-lis Tassel 2

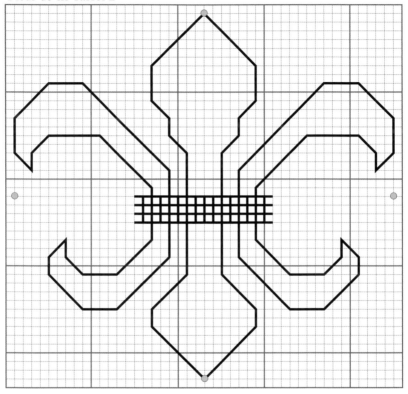

GIVE THANKS PILLOW

MATERIALS TO GATHER

- 6" x 8" 28-count natural linen
- 6" x 8" backing fabric
- Embroidery scissors
- Cord as desired
- Needles:
  Beading
  Size 24 tapestry
- Polyester stuffing

- Size 8 seed beads, copper with silver lining (7)
- Threads:
  Madeira #2006, dark brown (1 skein)
  Madeira #2002, orange (1 skein)
  Madeira #1509, sage green (1 skein)
  Madeira #1405, dk. green (1 skein)

INSTRUCTIONS

Finished size: 1" x 3¾"

Note: For stitch types and placements, see the project code and charts on page 49. One square of graphed chart represents 2 threads of linen.

1. Begin at the center of the design. Backstitch the lettering over 2 threads with 2 strands of dark brown as shown. Refer to Backstitch on page 16.

2. Vertically spider-stitch the pumpkin with 4 strands of orange as shown. *Note: The top of the pumpkin has 2 horizontal long stitches in the same orange with the same 4 strands.* Refer to Spider Stitch on page 19. Stitch the first stitch as an arch over 8 threads.

3. Stitch 4 diagonal long stitches for the stem with 4 strands of sage green. Refer to Long Stitch on page 18. Stitch the shorter orange horizontal long stitch over 6 threads. *Note: This stitch will cover the base of the stem.*

4. Backstitch the squiggly vine coming off of the pumpkin over 2 threads with 1 strand of dk. brown as shown.

5. Using the bead attachment stitch, attach copper beads as shown. Refer to Bead Attachment Stitch on page 16.

6. Sew cord to the linen. Place the right side of the linen and the right side of the backing fabric together, then long-stitch the sides together, leaving a 3" opening at bottom.

7. Turn the pillow right side out, stuff with polyester, and stitch the opening closed.

Stitch count: 44 x 16

Madeira Floss					
	XS	**BS**	**BD**	**LS**	**SP**
202	⊠				‖‖‖‖
1509				╲	
1405		⌐		⋙	
2006		⌐			
Copper			●		

Top Left   Give Thanks Pillow

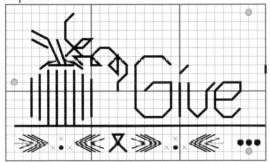

Give Thanks Pillow   Top Right

FLORAL BRACELET

MATERIALS TO GATHER

- 5" x 12" 32-count cream linen
- 7" metal link bracelet base
- 5mm crystals (44)
  Note: Model is shown with the following crystal colors: alexandrite, clear crystal, lt. sapphire, lt. yellow, peridot, rose, and topaz.
- Clear tacky glue

- Embroidery scissors
- Size 24 metal half-ball button covers (11)
- Size 26 tapestry needle
- Threads:
  Clear beading (1 skein)
  Madeira cotton #1205, green (1 skein)

INSTRUCTIONS

Finished size: 7"

Note: The bracelet is a standard 7" in length and requires 11 buttons to complete. The bracelet may be shortened or lengthened if necessary. To shorten, simply remove one link. To lengthen, it would require a second bracelet, then add the links necessary to fit your wrist.

1. Leaf-stitch four stitches branching out in four directions over 1 thread, with 3 strands of green. Refer to Leaf Stitch on page 18.

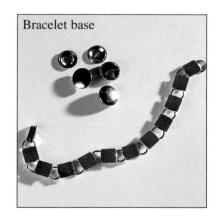

Bracelet base

50

2. Using bead attachment stitch, attach crystals to the fabric with the clear beading thread. Refer to Bead Attachment Stitch on page 16.

Step 2

3. Stitch each button design, then cut each design from the fabric in 1½" circle.

4. *Note: The metal button cover comes in two parts. One is the button cap with teeth and the other is the button disk that secures the fabric in place. The button cap has a shank which would allow you to use this as a button by sewing it onto a garment. For the button bracelet, the shank is not needed. Simply squeeze the shank together, it will pop out of the cap. Remove the shanks from all of the button caps.* To cover each button, center the stitched design over the cap. Wrap the fabric around the cap and attach the fabric to the teeth. If it needs recentering, lift from the teeth and recenter. Trim away excess fabric around the button, leaving just enough fabric to tuck into the cap.

5. Push the disk into the back of the cap. *Note: The disk will pop into place, securing and finishing the button.*

6. Glue the buttons onto the flat links of the bracelet.

Step 6

English Knot Garden

MATERIALS TO GATHER

- 5½" x 3¾" foam-core board

- 10" x 8" 28-count platinum linen

- Compressed quilt batting

- Embroidery scissors

- Size 24 tapestry needle

- Threads:
  ColorWash Japanese silk
  #589 (1 bobbin)
  Madeira cotton #0712,
  purple (1 skein)
  Madeira cotton #1105,
  lt. blue (1 skein)
  Madeira cotton #1311,
  med. green (1 skein)
  Madeira cotton #1314,
  dk. green (1 skein)
  Madeira cotton #1412,
  true green (1 skein)
  Madeira cotton #1604,
  lt. green (1 skein)
  Madeira cotton #1707,
  teal green (1 skein)
  Madeira cotton #2006,
  brown (1 skein)
  Madeira cotton #2206
  gold (1 skein)
  Madeira cotton #2310,
  terra-cotta (1 skein)
  Madeira cotton #2401,
  white (1 skein)
  Madeira cotton #2507,
  green (1 skein)
  Madeira cotton #2605
  peach (1 skein)
  Rainbow blending
  #R000 (1 bobbin)
  Rainbow blending
  #R115 (1 bobbin)
  Rainbow blending
  #R403 (1 bobbin)
  Rainbow blending
  #R705 (1 bobbin)

- Wooden box with
  5½" x 3¾" frame opening

Finished size: 5¼" x 3½"

Note: For stitch types and placements, see the project code and charts on pages 56–58. Each square of the graphed charts represents 2 threads of linen.

1. Begin at center of design. Cross-stitch with 2 strands of cotton as shown. Refer to Cross-stitch on page 17.

2. Backstitch with 1 strand of brown, over 2 threads unless otherwise indicated as shown. Refer to Backstitch on page 16.

3. Stitch Smyrna crosses along the outside border along fence over 4 threads with 4 strands of white as shown. Refer to Smyrna crosses on page 19. *Note: These are along both sides and across the back of the garden.*

4. Center floral bed at center back of garden. Planted in a checker-board style, stitch Smyrna crosses over 4 threads with 4 strands of lt. green as shown.

5. Stitch Smyrna crosses in the four corners of the center of garden over 4 threads with 4 strands of dk. green as shown.

6. Stitch Smyrna crosses to the left and right sides of the center garden over 4 threads with 4 strands of med. green as shown.

7. Stitch 4 Smyrna crosses in a row to the left and right sides of the center garden over 4 threads with 4 strands of med. green.

8. Place a piece of compressed quilt batting on top of the foam-core board to create padding. Cut the batting to the same size as the board. Do not wrap around the edges.

9. Place the stitched design on top of the batting and wrap the stitching fabric around to the back side. Using a long piece of thread and needle, stitch back and forth, side to side, like lac-ing a shoe while pulling and centering as you go. Insert in frame of box.

Madeira Floss

	XS	BS	FK	FS	SC	LF	SP	CS	SX
2401	·	⌐							✳
{ 2401 *R000	−								
2206			♥						
{ 2206 *R403	◇								
2605	∴								
2310	▲								
{ 0712 *R705	·|								
0712									✳
{ 1105 *R115	○								
1604	+								✳
1311	◑			↓	▨				✳
1412	N					⟫			
1314	★								✳
{ 1707 2507	□								
1707							✳	▨	
**589	E								
2006	■	⌐							

*GlissenGloss Rainbow Blending Thread
**GlissenGloss ColorWash Japanese Silk

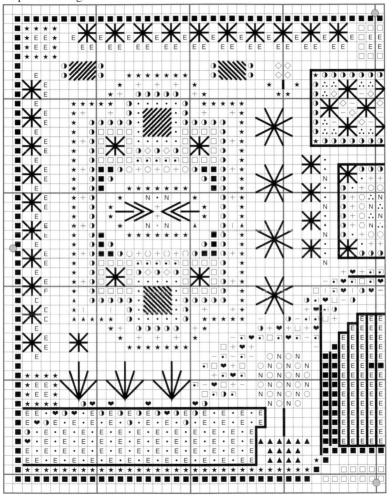

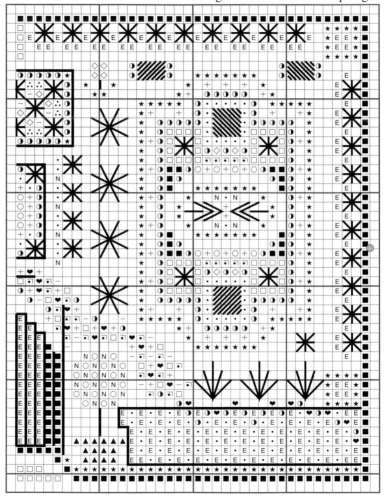

58

Garden Clock

- 1¾" x 4½" foam-core board
- 6" x 9" 28-count natural linen
- Compressed quilt batting
- Embroidery scissors
- Size 24 tapestry needle
- Threads:
  Madeira cotton #0902, lavender (1 skein)
  Madeira cotton #1310, lt. green (1 skein)
  Madeira cotton #1406, bright green (1 skein)
  Madeira cotton #1703, lt. teal green (1 skein)
  Madeira cotton #1705, dk. teal green (1 skein)

  Madeira cotton #1904, dk. gray brown (1 skein)
  Madeira cotton #2006, dk. chocolate brown (1 skein)
  Madeira cotton #2204, gold (1 skein)
  Madeira cotton #2303, copper (1 skein)
  Madeira cotton #2310, terra-cotta (1 skein)
  Madeira cotton #2404, ecru (1 skein)
  Madeira cotton #2609, raspberry (1 skein)

- Wooden clock with 1¾" x 4½" frame opening at clock base

Finished size: 1¾" x 4½"

Note: For stitch types and placements, see the project code and charts on pages 60 and 62. Each square of the graphed chart represents 2 threads of linen.

1. Begin at center of design. Cross-stitch over 2 threads of linen with 2 strands as shown. Refer to Cross-stitch on page 17.

2. Backstitch with 1 strand as shown. Refer to Backstitch on page 16.

3. Rice-stitch in upper-left and upper-right beds. Refer to Rice Stitch on page 18.

4. Upright cross-stitch down center of cobble stones with 2 strands of lt. green.

5. Stitch tied oblong cross-stitch in upper-center bed. Refer to Tied Oblong Cross-stitch on page 19.

6. Place a piece of compressed quilt batting on top of the foam-core board to create padding. Cut the batting to the same size as the board. Do not wrap around the edges.

7. Place the stitching on top of the batting and wrap the stitching fabric around to the back side. Using a long piece of thread and needle, stitch back and forth, side to side, like lacing a shoe while pulling and centering as you go. Insert in frame opening at clock base.

Stitch count: 24 x 64

Madeira Floss	XS	BS	RS	OX
Ecru	⊞	⌐		
2204	▽			
2310	∴			
2609	E			
0902	★			
1310	◇		✖	
1406	●			
1703	⊡			✗
1705	N	⌐		
2303	✕	⌐		
2006	▼	⌐		
1904		⌐		

Garden Clock

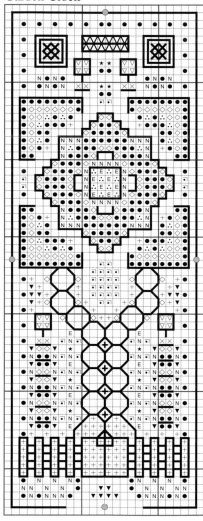

DRAGONFLY

MATERIALS TO GATHER

- 4" embroidery hoop
- 5" sq. sheer fabric
- 26-gauge wires:
  10" black
  18" white
- Beads:
  ¼" x ½" shades of green
  for dragonfly's body (3)
  ¼" dia. antique gold for
  tail (3)

Size 8 bronze beads
  for spacers (8)
Size 11 brown beads for
  head and tail (11)

- Embroidery scissors
- Size 26 tapestry needle
- Thread:
  Madeira cotton #1910,
  taupe (1 skein)
- Wire cutters

INSTRUCTIONS

1. Stretch the sheer fabric over embroidery hoop. Cut the white wire in half. Shape each piece of the wire into the shape of the wings.

2. Buttonhole-stitch, the wire to the sheer fabric with 1 strand of taupe. Refer to Buttonhole Stitch on page 16.

3. Cut out the wings. Twist the wire ends together to join both the wings.

4. String 1 brown bead to the center of the black wire. Fold the wire in half.

5. With both ends of the wire together, string 4 more brown beads over both wires. Continue stringing over both wire ends. String 1 bronze, 1 brown, 1 bronze, 1 brown, 1 bronze, 1 brown beads. String 2–3 decorative beads, alternating with

the bronze beads for the tail. String 3 large body beads, alternating with the bronze beads. After the last body bead, string 1 brown bead, then 1 bronze bead.

6. Attach the sheer wings by twisting the wire of the wings around the black dragonfly wire between the body beads.

7. String 2 brown beads, 1 on each black wire, creating the dragonfly's eyes. Twist the wires to tighten all of the beads that have been strung into place. Thread the wires back through the eye beads to secure. Twist again, creating the antennae. Shape and trim as desired.

DOGWOOD CLIP

- 4" embroidery hoop
- 8" sq. off-white muslin fabric
- 5mm crystals:
  lt. rose (3)
  lt. topaz (4)
- 26-gauge wires:
  Beige, soft pink, or white for dogwood bracts (1 yd)
  Dk. green or black for dogwood leaf (¾ yd)
- Binder clip
- Embroidery scissors
- Hot-glue gun/glue sticks

- Needles:
  Beading
  Size 24 tapestry
- Threads:
  Clear beading (1 yd)
  ColorWash Japanese silk #574, variegated beige to soft rose (1 bobbin)
  Madeira cotton #1205, teal green (1 skein)
  Madeira cotton #1406, med. green (1 skein)
  Madeira cotton #1507, dk. green (1 skein)
- Wire cutters

Note: The dogwood flower and leaf are stitched with the traditional stumpwork technique of dimensional embroidery.

1. Stretch the muslin fabric over embroidery hoop. Stitch the four dogwood bracts. *Note: These showy bracts are often mistaken as petals.*

65

2. Cut the beige, soft pink, or white wire into four equal pieces. Shape the wire into the bract shape as shown in Bract Pattern above. Lay the wire onto the muslin.

Bract Pattern

3. Couch-stitch the wire to the fabric. Refer to Couch Stitch on page 17. Make the couching stitches as invisible as possible by taking the needle up and down through the same hole in the muslin fabric. Use 1 strand of variegated silk.

4. Fill in each bract with long and short satin stitches with 6 strands variegated silk, using the following method. Refer to Satin Stitch on page 19.
    a. Start at the outer edge of the top of the bract. Work the first row, alternating long and short satin stitches. Follow the contours of the shape to be filled. Keep stitches close together so that fabric is not visible.

    b. On the next row, fit stitches of equal length into spaces left by short stitches in previous row. On this second and subsequent rows of stitches, bring the needle and thread up a short distance away from the first short stitch, then take the thread through the end of this stitch and back into the background fabric. Continue until shape is filled.

5. Start the wire at the base of the bracts. Leave approximately a 2" tail of wire at the start and at the end to be used later when assembling the dogwood.

6. Buttonhole-stitch a row over the wire with 4 strands of variegated silk. Refer to Buttonhole Stitch on page 16. Start at the base of the petal and work around the shape. Do not cut off the tail of the thread, this can be used when putting the bracts together.

7. Cut around the outside edge of the bract, cutting as close as possible to the buttonhole stitches without cutting the stitches. *Note: If you make an unexpected cut, coat the edge with a tiny touch of tacky glue.*

8. Repeat this same technique in stitching and finishing the dogwood leaf. See Leaf Pattern below. *Note: The leaf is stitched with a blend of the three greens.* Fill your needle with 1 strand of color teal green, plus 1 strand of med. green, plus 1 strand of dk. green. Stitch the long and short

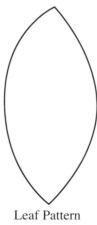

Leaf Pattern

satin stitches and the buttonhole stitches with this same blend.

9. Assemble the dogwood bracts by twisting the wires together on the back side. Accent the center of the flower with the 5mm crystals, using the following method:

   a. Thread 6 crystals together, alternating colors. Thread back through all of the crystals and pull together, creating a circle.

   b. Place the last crystal at the center of the circle. Thread back through the crystals one more time to secure. Sew this cluster of crystals to the center of the dogwood flower.

   c. Twist the leaf in place under the flower blossom.

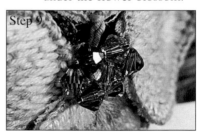

Step 9

10. Hot-glue the dogwood flower to a binder clip.

CORNER BOOKMARK

MATERIALS TO GATHER

- ½"-wide sheer white ribbon (24")
- 7" sq. backing fabric
- 9" sq. 22-count white even-weave fabric
- Embroidery scissors

- Size 24 tapestry needle
- Threads:
  DMC pearl cotton size 5, white (1 skein)
  DMC pearl cotton size 8, white (1 skein)
- Tweezers

INSTRUCTIONS

Finished size: 5" sq.

Notes: For stitch types and placements, see the project code and charts on pages 70–72. Each square of the graphed chart represents 2 threads of even-weave fabric.

The back side of bookmark goes over the corner of a book to mark pages. Decorative front panel rests on the front of the book.

1. Long-stitch the inside scalloped edge area with size 5 pearl cotton as shown. Refer to Long Stitch on page 18.

2. Buttonhole-stitch the outside scalloped area with size 8 pearl cotton as shown. Refer to Buttonhole Stitch on page 16.

3. Cross-stitch the symbol of black dots over 2 threads as shown. Refer to Cross-stitch on page 17.

4. Stitch Smyrna crosses for the border design as shown. Refer to Smyrna cross-stitch on page 19.

5. Eyelet-stitch the heart design. Refer to Eyelet Stitch on page 17.

6. Vertical-long-stitch the kloster blocks over 4 threads as shown. Refer to Kloster Blocks on

page 18. *Note: Every kloster block must have an opposite kloster block across the motif.*

7. Once the stitching is complete, cut out the center of the kloster blocks, holding the scissors to the left side of the kloster block. Cut only those threads perpendicular to the long stitches of the kloster block. *Note: Do not cut parallel to the long stitches.* Use tweezers to remove threads.

8. Buttonhole-stitch the outside edge with size 8 pearl cotton over 2 threads as shown. Once the buttonhole-stitching is complete, cut away excess fabric right up to the stitching without cutting into the stitching to create the scalloped edge.

9. Place backing fabric onto the back side of stitched design. Turn edges of backing fabric under ½" on all sides and stitch pieces together, leaving scalloped edge open. *Note: The scalloped edge slips over the book pages.*

10. Thread ribbon through open kloster blocks as desired and tie ends into a bow.

Stitch count: 61 x 61

DMC Pearl Cotton						
	XS	**SX**	**ES**	**LS**	**BH**	**KB**
White #5	•	✳	✳	╲╲		▦
White #8					‖‖‖	

Top Left   Corner Bookmark

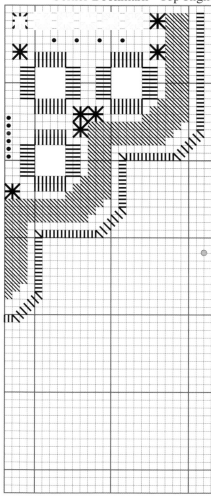

STRAWBERRY POTPOURRI

- 1" x 2" red felt
- 4" embroidery hoop
- 5" sq. 25-count white even-weave
- Copier paper
- Needles:
  Beading
  Size 24 tapestry
- Pencil
- Scissors:
  Craft
  Embroidery
- Size 11 seed beads tricut dk. green (180)
  Note: A 10" string of the same beads can be used.

- Size 60 half-ball metal button
- Straight pins
- Sugar shaker
- Tacky glue
- Threads:
  Madeira cotton #0602, strawberry red (1 skein)
  Madeira cotton #1707, leaf green (1 skein)
  Rainbow metallic blending #R407 (1 yd)

Finished size: 1"

Note: For stitch types and placements, see the project code and charts on pages 78–79. Each square of the graphed chart represents 1 fabric thread.

1. Backstitch the outline of the strawberry with 1 strand of strawberry red as shown. Refer to Backstitch on page 16.

2. Using a pencil, trace the Strawberry Patterns below onto the copier paper.

Strawberry Patterns

3. Using craft scissors, cut out the templates. Pin the templates onto felt and cut out the designs.

4. To pad the strawberry, long-stitch the small-sized design piece of felt onto the even-weave fabric. Refer to Long Stitch on page 18.

5. Long-stitch the middle-sized design piece over the small-sized design piece. Repeat for the large-sized design piece as shown on Strawberry Potpourri 2 on page 78. *Note: The strawberry's edges should fall within the edges of the backstitching. If you cannot see the backstitches, trim the felt. For best results, strip all threads, separate, and repad the strawberry.*

6. Stitch horizontal and long sating stitches in and out of every hole, side to side with all strands of red as shown on Strawberry Potpourri 3 on page 78. Refer to Satin Stitch on page 18. *Note: These stitches are considered the padding stitches and will not be seen.*

7. Stitch vertical horizontal satin stitches with the same strands of red as shown on Strawberry Potpourri 4 on page 78 *Note: These stitches are the final layer and are considered the finishing stitches. Take care to lay the stitches smoothly.*

8. Stitch short vertical long stitches over the red satin stitches to create the strawberry's seeds. Refer to Strawberry Potpourri 5 on page 79 for approximate placement of seeds.

9. Turkeywork-stitch the leaf cap with 4 strands of green as shown on Strawberry Potpourri 6 on page 79. Refer to

Turkeywork Stitch on page 19. *Note: The Turkeywork loops should be approximately ⅛"–¼" in length. The loops remain uncut. When finished, fluff the loops to spread them.*

Step 9

10. Using the metal half-ball button as a template, cut out the design 1" larger around than the metal button. *Note: It is better to cut the circle a little larger at first. Additional trimming may always be done.*

11. Squeeze the shank together, it will pop out of the cap. Remove the shank from the button cap and discard. *Note: This will allow the button to be glued on a flat surface.*

12. Center the stitched design over the cap. Wrap the fabric around the cap and attach the fabric to the teeth. If it needs recentering, lift from the teeth and recenter. Trim excess fabric if necessary, tuck remainder of the fabric into the cap. Push the disk into the back of the cap. *Note: This disk will pop into place securing and finishing the button.*

13. Glue the button to the top of a sugar shaker.

14. Embellish with beads glued to the outside edge of the button.

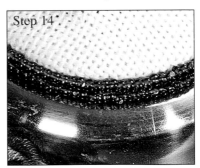

Step 14

Stitch count: 18 x 17

Madeira Floss					
	BS	SS	SS	LS	TW
0602	⌐	|	—		
*R407				▮	
1707					⬭
* Rainbow Blending Thread					

Strawberry Potpourri 1

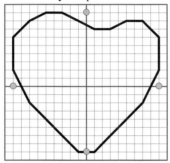

Strawberry Potpourri 2

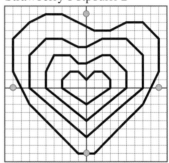

Strawberry Potpourri 3

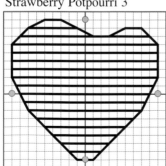

Strawberry Potpourri 4

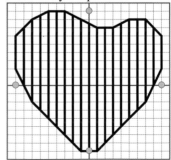

Strawberry Potpourri 5

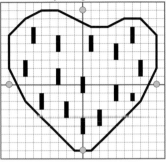

Strawberry Potpourri 6

HOLLY NAPKIN RING

MATERIALS TO GATHER
- 5" embroidery hoop
- 5" x 8" 32-count platinum linen
  Note: Fabric size needed depends on napkin ring's diameter.
- 6" sq. holly green organza
- 26-gauge black wire (18")
- Embroidery scissors
- Napkin ring
- Needles:
  Beading
  Size 24 tapestry

- Size 11 seed beads:
  Dk. green (80)
  Iridescent green (19)
- Tacky glue
- Threads:
  Madeira cotton #0512, deep red (1 skein)
  Madeira cotton #1314, dk. green (1 skein)
  Madeira metallic #9805, antique gold (1 skein)
- Wire cutters

INSTRUCTIONS
Finished size: 1¼"

1. Reverse-spider-stitch the three holly berries with 3 strands of deep red onto the linen. Refer to Spider Stitch on page 19.

Step 1

Note: The reverse-spider stitch begins the same as the spider stitch, then additional

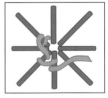

threads are wrapped over 2 spokes, then under 1. The finished stitch has the appearance of solid stitches in a circular motion.

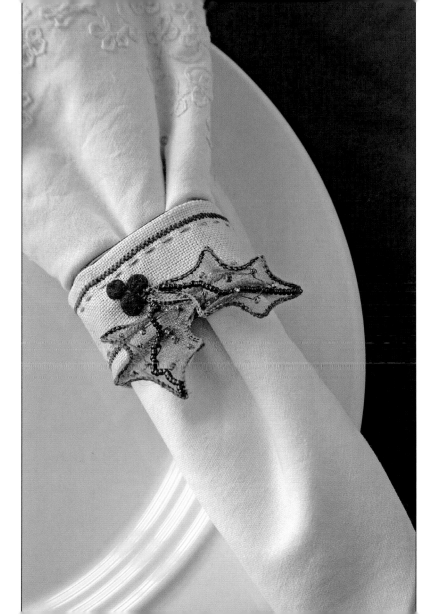

2. Stitch the border on each side of linen long enough to wrap around the napkin ring as follows:

   a. Backstitch the inside row over 4 threads, skip 4 threads, backstitch over 4, skip, etc., as shown. Refer to Backstitch on page 16.

   b. Cross-stitch the outside row over 2 threads with strands of dk. green as shown. Refer to Cross-stitch on page 17.

3. Stitch leaves on organza fabric.

4. Cut wire in half. Mold and shape the wire as shown in Leaf Pattern. Place sheer fabric into hoop. *Note: This is very important, stretching the sheer fabric will give you a surface on which to work.*

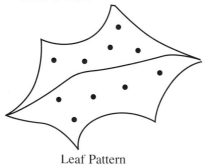

Leaf Pattern

5. Lay the molded wire on top of the sheer fabric. Buttonhole-stitch the wire to the sheer fabric with 2 strands of dk. green for first leaf. Refer to Buttonhole Stitch on page 16. Stitch over the wire and down through the sheer fabric. Space each buttonhole stitch along the wire approximately 1/16"–1/8" apart.

6. Repeat for the second leaf in the same manner. Space the two leaves apart on the sheer fabric.

7. Using bead attachment stitch, attach beads as shown. Refer to Bead Attachment on page 16.

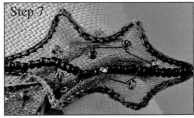

Step 7

8. Fold the stitched fabric edges under and glue finished design to napkin ring.

PERSIAN RUG

- 7" x 8" 28-count cream linen

- Embroidery scissors

- Size 24 tapestry needle

- Smooth thin cardboard

- Threads:
  Madeira #0401, brick red (1 skein)
  Madeira #1704, teal green (1 skein)
  Madeira #1712, colonial blue (1 skein)
  Madeira #2209, gold (1 skein)
  Madeira #2400, black (1 skein)
  Madeira #2404, ecru (1 skein)

Finished size: 3½" x 5"

Note: For stitch types and placements, see the project code and charts on pages 85–87. Each square of the graphed chart represents 2 threads of linen.

1. Begin at the center of the design. Cross-stitch with 2 strands as shown. Refer to Cross-stitch on page 17.

2. Backstitch with 1 strand as shown. Refer to Backstitch on page 16.

3. Turn top and bottom edges under, leaving two rows of linen showing on top and bottom. Turn both side edges under right next to the backstitching.

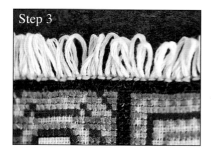
Step 3

Stitch count: 50 x 56

Madeira Floss		
	XS	**BS**
2209	△	
0401	✛	
1712	▼	
1704	▢	
2400	●	⌐

4. Holding the smooth thin cardboard up to the top edge, wrap the loops of the Turkeywork over the cardboard.

5. When an entire row of Turkeywork is complete, slide the guide out of the loops. Repeat for bottom edge.

Tip: The Turkeywork loops may be cut open and trimmed or left as loops. The loops can also be randomly trimmed, creating more texture. An eyebrow brush can be used for combing the cut loop if necessary.

Top Left   Persian Rug

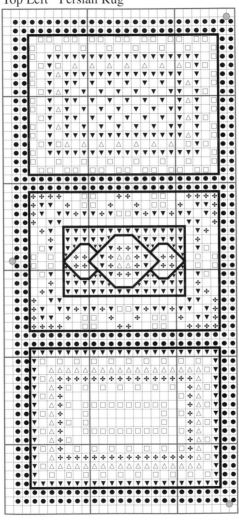

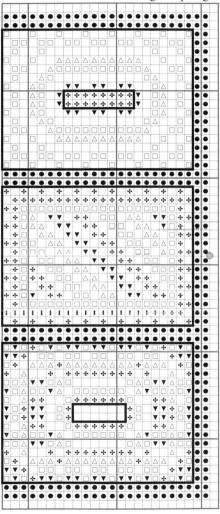

FRIENDS PILLOW

MATERIALS TO GATHER

- 8" x 12" 28-count
  stone even-weave fabric

- 8" x 12" backing fabric

- Embroidery scissors

- Cord as desired

- Polyester stuffing

- Size 26 tapestry needle

- Threads:
  Madeira cotton #2304,
    chocolate brown
    (1 skein)
  Madeira metallic #482,
    variegated copper
    (1 bobbin)

INSTRUCTIONS

Finished size: 2½" x 7"

Note: For stitch types and placements, see the project code and charts on pages 90–91. Each square of the graphed chart represents 2 threads of linen.

1. Cross-stitch entire saying over 2 threads of the linen with 1 strand of chocolate brown plus 1 strand of metallic copper as shown. Refer to Cross-stitch on page 17.

2. Stitch cord to finished cross-stitch fabric.

3. Place the right side of the stitched fabric and the right side of the backing fabric together. Stitch the sides together, leaving a 3" opening for stuffing.

4. Turn the pillow right sides out, stuff with polyester and stitch the opening closed.

Stitch count: 110 x 40

Madeira Floss	
	XS
{ 2304 *482	■
*Madeira Variegated Copper	

Top Left   Friends Pillow

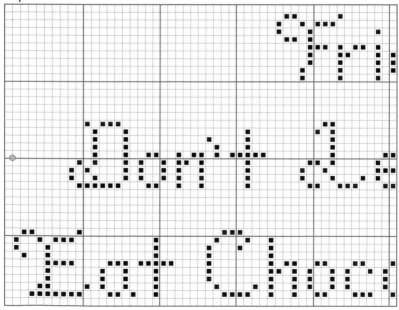

Note: As with any project in this
book, feel free to change the color and
type of thread or fabric used. You may
also cross-stitch any desired saying
onto the fabric.

Friends Pillow   Top Right

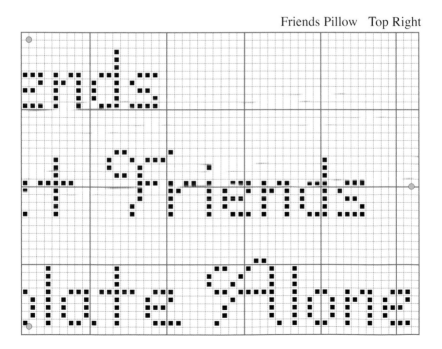

The above saying was stitched on a piece of 9" x 11" 28-count flax linen. The design has 1¼" of linen around the saying. The stitched fabric edges have been turned under and tacked onto the pillow.

The four paw prints were cross-stitched on 3" squares. Each paw print has been centered and attached onto size 45 metal half-ball button covers. These button covers were sewn onto the four corners of the cross-stitched saying.

Liz Turner Diehl finds inspiration in the surroundings at her home. The beaches and mountains of Oregon give an atmosphere that spawns creativity. Liz learned to needlepoint as a young girl in Kansas. Saturday nights brought together Liz and her Grandmother, needlepointing and watching Lawrence Welk. She has fond memories of that special time.

Her formal training is in music. It was a difficult choice for Liz between music and art. For Liz, they go hand in hand. Her needlework career spans 30 years from the early days of working in a needlework shop to owning a retail needlework shop to teaching needlework throughout the country and internationally and owning and operating a needlework design company. Today, Liz continues to fill her life with music and art and family. She plays bass and flute in a Steel Drum Band, publishes her own needlework designs, and is a partner in the retail consumer show "Stitching Festival."

Madeira
Conversion Chart

MADEIRA	DMC	MADEIRA	DMC	MADEIRA	DMC
0109	726	1406	3345	2209	729
0510	321	1412	905	2210	680
0512	816	1507	936	2303	975
0602	3685	1509	3052	2304	400
0706	917	1558	1003	2310	3778
0707	718	1604	772	2400	310
0712	553	1703	502	2404	Ecru
0902	340	1705	500	2401	B5200
1011	825	1707	926	2505	3808
1105	519	1904	3021	2506	3765
1205	561	1910	842	2507	3808
1214	911	2114	830	2605	3779
1302	910	2203	729	2609	3803
1310	368	2006	898	9805	5014
1311	320	2204	729		
1314	890	2206	3046		

METRIC CONVERSION CHART

inches to millimeters and centimeters
(mm-millimeters, cm-centimeters)

inches	mm	cm	inches	cm	inches	cm
⅛	3	0.3	11	27.9	31	78.7
¼	6	0.6	12	30.5	32	81.3
⅜	10	1.0	13	33.0	33	83.8
½	13	1.3	14	35.6	34	86.4
⅝	16	1.6	15	38.1	35	88.9
¾	19	1.9	16	40.6	36	91.4
⅞	22	2.2	17	43.2	37	94.0
1	25	2.5	18	45.7	38	96.5
1¼	32	3.2	19	48.3	39	99.1
1½	38	3.8	20	50.8	40	101.6
1¾	44	4.4	21	53.3	41	104.1
2	51	5.1	22	55.9	42	106.7
3	76	7.6	23	58.4	43	109.2
4	102	10.2	24	61.0	44	111.8
5	127	12.7	25	63.5	45	114.3
6	152	15.2	26	66.0	46	116.8
7	178	17.8	27	68.6	47	119.4
8	203	20.3	28	71.1	48	121.9
9	229	22.9	29	73.7	49	124.5
10	254	25.4	30	76.2	50	127.0

INDEX